ORDINARY TIME

ORDINARY TIME

Poems

Paul Mariani

SL/.NT
BOOKS

ORDINARY TIME
Poems

Slant Books
P.O. Box 60295
Seattle, WA 98160

www.slantbooks.com

HARDCOVER ISBN: 978-1-63982-031-3
PAPERBACK ISBN: 978-1-63982-030-6
EBOOK ISBN: 978-1-63982-032-0

Cataloguing-in-Publication data:

Names: Mariani, Paul.

Title: Ordinary time : poems / Paul Mariani.

Description: Seattle, WA: Slant Books, 2020

Identifiers: ISBN 978-1-63982-031-3 (hardcover) | ISBN 978-1-63982-030-6 (paperback) | ISBN 978-1-63982-032-0 (ebook)

Subjects: LCSH: Poetry

Classification: PS3563.A6543 O73 2020 (print) | PS3563.A6543 (ebook)

Manufactured in the U.S.A.   10/05/21

For Eileen, always there. Always there.

Contents

III

IV

I

DE PROFUNDIS

And the Spirit of God was hovering over the face of the waters.

A blank slate, an empty canvas, that sheet
of foolscap eight and a half by eleven long.
Bob Creeley—late minimalist,
hip puritan, wiping at his one good

eye—told me once was how a poem began.
Began, because there was no other choice.
And young James Franco, telling me how
he'd tried to recreate what Hart Crane

had done by staring at his own blank page
there on that Olivetti. He was recalling
something Ed Harris had once said:
how he wished he'd kept those two

minutes in the film he was making, where
Jackson Pollock stares unblinking into
the white canvas at the nothing that is there,
not unlike the Creator God who once stared

into the darkness covering the face, if face
it was, given the way the language works—
or doesn't—that seems to call us from those depths.
That is, until the Spirit, the Arch Breath,

call it the Wind if you will, whipped over
those waters, as over some blank black canvas.
And, in time (if there was time back then)
God said, Let there be light. And like that,

like a switch turning on, there was light,
and the Lord saw it and called it good. And
where nothing was (if non-being can be said
to be) the trumpet sound of sound itself

began to sound. And it was good. And words
followed: the multifoliate pulse of Pythagorean
sound. Music is its name, what the ancients,
who seemed to know knew better than

we know (if we know anything at all)
called the Music of the Spheres. Then
lines. Lines of verse. Lines of paint as now
Pollock's brush begins to swerve down

and then across the canvas. And it was good.
Oh, it was very good, for as Issho says,
we must learn to live as waves, each of us unique,
but part, always part, of the ocean from which

we came and to which we must return:
a face of water that stares into a face of water
across which the Wind must always wave its way.
And then it's back once more to that blank slate

that began these lines: the empty canvas
which seems to taunt the one who dares
to stare upon its face until you catch it staring
unblinking back into the blank face of the beholder.

SILVER MOON

Old moon rising over the Hotel David,
silvering the storied streets of Jerusalem.
Holy city, alleluia! Holy city.
Adolescent moon waving seaward beyond
Key West, glittering the palm-swayed beaches.
Acetylene moon, processing past Paterson's
brick silk mills as they drowsed
in the evening air, half aware of the steady
roar of the Great Falls, where we played among
the rusting iron fences when we were children.

Drunken moon, that night I drove my Beta
Sigma brothers through the Bronx streets
home to their apartments, swerving left, right,
left as I sang some inane insane song, and—
thanks to you, my watchdog Guardian
Angel—have lived to talk about it.

Somnolent moon high over El Capitan, where
once a grizzly snuffled outside our cabin,
the kids thank God asleep. Moon higher
still over the Wilbur Cross Parkway,
forming a refulgent silver lake as we drove
north toward Hartford and beyond.

Brother moon, Bre'r Moon, tangled
in a briar patch of clotheslines, an acrid sweetness
of baked tar coating the buckled roof
of my long-lost crumbling brownstone tenement
which once faced the beckoning diamond lights
of the Chrysler. Antediluvian moon, moon
older than Moses, older than Ashurbanipal,
than Adam even, you, the lesser light the Lord
created on the fourth day, silvering the earth.

Moon, dear moon, the comfort you bring

each time I catch you as you slowly process past,
left to right, but steadier than I was then,
royal moon choired by katydids, or peeking
through the glittered winter ice. Catch you, ah!,
whenever I climb the creaking stairs in darkness.
In truth, you seem to look down and wink at me
through the stained-glass window when I reach
the landing with its giant potted eucalyptus.

Oh I know they say you are a floating rock
pockmarked with shadow craters, half of you
forever hidden from us in darkness. Know too
there are black and white videos taken by men,
brave men surely, and all gone now, such is
our common fate, even for those few who reach
for stars, and who, half floating in their awkward
necessary lifelines, dream of touching you.

Moon, old moon, dear moon, I beg you
answer me when I call out to you,
as I have from the eerie hospital bed,
or over the lit dashboard of my car, or from
the north room where my love is sleeping now,
here next to me, as she has for fifty years
and more, constant companion, ancient
moon, as we go silvering on, alleluia.

O

the man's contrabasso seems to groan.
And O and O her medley seems to moan.

Music as feeling, then, not sound.
Music as so much more, at least this time round.

A cross, he thinks, between some blue-black
sigh of plainchant and the memory of those half-

heard river-haunted Mississippi blues.
Or a bridge of sorrows like some age-old bruise

cascading from the choiring shadows
in the upper loft: these crests and shallows,

these syllables that knife into his very marrow
as he kneels there in the pinewood pew below.

What to call this ache, this unearthly tremolo
of moans, these bubbling sibilants, this O and O

that has found him out and once again reminds him
of the empty O he is, as now the blank abyss within

gives way like some mountain glacier, just so,
and disappears into the yawning maw below

until at last it flutters dovelike down, this O,
and comes to nest, as on that day so long ago

when those who surely must have loved him
held his tiny forehead above the marble rim

and the kind cold waters of the Holy Ghost so
startled him he cried out with his own and infant O.

WHAT'S IN A NAME?

For K.B.

A paralyzing gelid vortex of a January morning.
He lay under the covers as the beckoning New Year's sun
began to manifest itself through the curtains of his bedroom
window, but unlike the busy old sun unwilling

to rise up and begin the day. His better half, it must be said,
was already dressed and downstairs, making
a fresh pot of coffee and—warming to it—baking
a batch or three of her delicious Irish soda bread.

Still, as the minutes floated on and floated by, he kept lying
there, trying to remember the first name or at least
the first letter or first syllable of the woman—a guess,
a hazard, a Matteo Ricci way of trying to remember, trying

to put a name and face together for her who would undergo
a partial hysterectomy that very morning. Well, loss
is loss is loss: a cross, a heavy double cross
to bear when names for people go under with the undertow

and names and things meant to stick fast to this or that
do-hickey thingamajig any handyman would know go
astray, along with the names of those dear to him, or so
it goes, he tries to tell himself. But the years accrete

along one's memory banks and names get buried under,
so that he wonders now if God would know just who
he was intent on praying for, but whose name refused to
reveal itself, vanishing, alas, alas, into the land of Wonder.

But surely the Ineffable would know exactly who
he meant to pray for? After all, what's in a name?
And how many, really, would undo the name
their loving parents gave them, or want to rate that slew

of echoic vocables on a scale of one to ten?
Did his old dog Sparky, gone these thirty years,
ever assent to be named the name he gave him? Tears,
for Sparky, *sunt lachrimae rerum,* as he remembers him.

And does God know us only by the names our parents gave us?
And is that how we will be known when we arrive
in or on or at the Empyrean? Or will our names survive
when death comes knocking at our door? And will that save us?

Which one of ten thousand languages, he wonders,
does God prefer to speak, if indeed he must surmise?
And do the angels speak there only with their eyes?
And if he rambles on with such questions will he blunder?

And are there really any answers? Still, doesn't God
call us by our names, as he called out to chastened Eve
and Adam to come out as they lay hidden in the leaves?
And didn't he call out to Samuel to come forward,

though he had to call him how many times? And didn't the Son,
rising fresh that first Easter morning, call Mary by her name,
when his blue-black body, charged now with iridescent flame,
came risen from the grave? Mary, Mary. Ask any woman

what she feels when she hears her beloved call
out to her by her name, a sound trilling like a bowstring
across the midriff of a plangent cello quivering
even as the music enters the silent mystery of it all?

Or ask the small boy cornered on one of those thousand name-
less city streets, the El rumbling and the faces gleaming
as they taunt him with kerosene and matches 'til he's screaming.
Ask him what he feels when he hears his mother calling out his name.

THE OPEN WINDOW
For Gregory Wolfe

In Pierre Bonnard's *The Open Window*
the artist looks outward from his modest
living room. It is summer, the heat
baking the orange on the grill-like wall.

To the right, a woman is resting in a chair,
escaping as she can the sizzling
midday air in which even her quizzical
black cat blurs in the irradiance of light.

Above her head: an open window
dotted with abstract fantails, beyond which
cool greens and cooler blues appear to beckon,
and where a dark cross winks in the shimmering sky.

An old man stands before an image
of the painting, gift of his grandson,
and which seems to whisper from across
the room where the old man will spend his final days.

Are those vines covering the frame
of some ruined house, he asks himself,
or tree limbs damasked against the sky?
And is what he stares at merely paint,

abstract form dissolving once more into
formlessness? Or is his eye transfixed
by a wheel of light swirling with all of love's
abandon about the resting woman, singing

something he alone can hear, a song
cut short by the shade that frames the window?
Still, there they are, beyond the fevered heat: those
beckoning greens, those cool and lucent blues.

HIGH TEA WITH MISS JULIANNA

"Begin at the beginning," the King said gravely,
"and go on till you come to the end: then stop."

In the land of the JubJub together they had tea.
High tea, one has to understand, six cups of imaginary
tea, the good Miss Julianna Frances, aged two
and a half, and her grandfather, sixty-four. "How *do*
you do this afternoon, Miss Julianna," he began,
good manners there in JubJub Land
being understood and *de rigueur* between
the Professor and his finical little Queen.
Sporting diapers beneath her summer dress,
she poured her airy tea in cups with such finesse
they might've been in Queen Victoria's drawing room
instead of in his modest parlor. "Might I presume
upon you, my lady dear, for yet another piece of cake?"
"Oh, sure," she too demurely said. "But let me bake
it first. It will only take one minute." I.e., one minute
in her understanding, for they had time within it
for another cup or two or four or six or three
of Miss Julianna's very best imaginary tea,
and time for her to sit upon his lap so he might read her
all about the Midnight Land of JubJub and then confer
together about the best way to pick the naughty dirts
from between their toes, or which of her many skirts
her dolly, coincidentally named for Daddy John,
should wear, and which chair he should sit upon
if Daddy John were to be invited to partake
of tea with them, together with a second piece of cake,
which was humming along just fine in the imaginary
oven in the slowly darkening room. High tea
on a Sunday afternoon at summer's end,
sweet credences of summer. How better to spend
an hour, a day, a year? And Alice leading down
the rabbit hole, and him following into JubJub town,
and all cares left behind now, as the little girl—who would
not be little long—beckoned towards the still-enchanted wood.

MISS JULIANNA REVISITED TWELVE YEARS ON

Flat blue sky and a seaweed sea composed
of moss and myrtle greens. Add two
thin brushstrokes for whitecaps in what
would be the distance. And there, facing you:
two faceless figures, both smiling perhaps.

One is a man—whitecap highlights deckling
his graying hair, a hint of shadow his only
other feature, his tee-shirt a monochrome of blue.
That would be you. The other is a little girl,
age three or so, in a lavender two-piece

bathing suit decked out with asterisk-like
rose pink purple stars, a little girl
so full of life, and whom he holds in both
his arms tight against his chest, as if
he had the power to keep her from all harm.

Somewhere, he hopes, a world much like the one
his granddaughter has painted here exists,
a world no one can ever tear from them.
And, if not that, oh, if not that, then at least a world
where he can always hold her in his heart.

SOPHIA

"You know I love you more than that, more
than anyone," you said, and said in such a way
that I believed you then, my dear, as to this day
I do. And what more could any grandpa ask for,

what with your innate grace (your middle name,
as wisdom is your first), and that radiance that flows
in your sweet gaze. Your Botticellian smile bestows
a sunrise goodness that few I think can ever claim.

I've meant to pen a poem for you for so long now.
Words harvested and kept for you alone, some token
of my love for the priceless pearl you are, spoken
from a heart which might, just might, convey (somehow)

a glimpse, a whisper of what I would—if I knew how,
if only I knew how—the love & peace & joy I feel
whenever I think of you. And then I think: she'll
know, my dear Sophia, as she knew then, as she knows now.

THE STONE MY GRANDSON GAVE ME

For Gavin at seven

Bright yellow, like his hair, and shadowed, the one side
flat so it could rest here on my desk, a simple fragment
of something bigger, something it seems now heaven-sent,
waiting for us on the sidewalk, where his blue eyes spied
it as we strolled together down the town's one wide
maple-lined street toward the old brick church, a boy bent
on racing down the length of the muddy grass embankment,
before charging up the massive neo-Georgian porticos to hide.

Jacob's angel, I thought to myself, being of that mind
that can glimpse—like you and you—the wondrous world around.
For you, he shouted, running up ahead. Call it something. A kind
of currency, money in the bank, something the very ground
had yielded up this day, anno domini, which the boy had signed:
a thing turned diamond before my eyes, as if waiting to be found.

GAVIN AT FOURTEEN

And just like that, in the stuttered blink of an eye,
seven years added to those first seven years,
and you're on your way, my boy. The tears, fears,
the cares, the grins, the jokes, the joys, the. . .And try
as I will, how can mere sounds and vocables that fly
each which way hope to catch your spirit that so cheers
your grandfather who grows more unsteady as he steers
himself around the kitchen table with his comic sigh?

How many times we've watched you out on the field
pitching that sly knuckleball of yours, the batter intent
on slamming one out into the crowd to win the game.
Or watched you on the stage, a Mandarin conman wield-
ing power, though, being you, you'd rather have sent
a comic line sailing to please the crowd. If fame were all the same.

SIXTH-GRADE HOCKEY ON THE GREENFIELD RINK

Five then four for a ninety-second penalty
then five again down at the far end
then a hurricane of green and white
hurling this way with a pass a pivot
then what seems a pas de deux then
another pass as the puck whacks against
the see-through plastic barrier and there's
the hawkeyed Griff modest (as always)
and steady as a chess knight skating back
back then floating sideways as the puck wheels
faster than my eyes can follow and now
he's got it and he's heading for their goalie
a kid so big so geared up with his blocker
in his right and his trapper in his left suited up
in his *Halloween* flick death-white face mask
so that you have to wonder how a puck slapped
even at a hundred miles an hour could ever
get past that dragon at the gate as one then two
blue blurs come closing in on him intent only
on stealing back that speck that priceless puck
at any cost as now the Griffer shifts then passes
then retrieves the spheroid thing and now
he feints off to the left then slams it there
yes there right there into the corner that
too late squeezes shut and bam!
And like that it's 1-0 and someone's father
is banging on the plastic barrier as shouts
go roaring up from the metal bleachers
and Griffer's grandpa's going *Woo hoo!* before
he remembers to compose himself once more.

And with that the game goes on again
and soon the players morph into other kids
who look like Griff but with different strides
and numbers on their backs as some skate out
though the team door and some skate in.
And soon the kids on the other team
do their quid pro quos to even up the score.

And so it goes, week in week out the winter
through, a sport you never thought to follow
until your grandson took it up, practicing it
even in his living room, where his parents
have let him set up a net on the ancient
wooden farmhouse floor into which he slams
the puck again and then again hour after hour
while good old Hudson shakes himself
then shuffles off into the other room. A game
where Griffin seems to know all the stats
and teams and players and even dreams about
a world where grim opponents keep coming
for him, and where he must somehow face
the white-masked monster and send the missive
he's been charged with wheeling through.

LITTLE ANTHONY LEADS HIS MASSIVE HOUND ABOUT

He seems to show no fear, my grandson,
when he takes the family's massive
pitch black lab by the collar and leads him
out back into the yard, though Coal—
the clever moniker they gave him as a pup—
is now a head taller and outweighs Anthony
by thirty pounds and muscles in
with that wet nose of his on everything
like some dark angel who just because
he can means to have his way, as these marks
along my arms and wrists will show.

Surely there's a parable here for us.
At least the Book of Revelations
seems to say there is, along with Milton's
fallen angels. When he was only five
I watched in wonder as he assembled
a thousand-piece Lego castle in a scant
two hours. I have watched him bake
Irish soda bread to perfection with his mother
and taunt his older sisters to the point of tears,
though they could have stuffed him in a blanket
and set him on the curb had they thought of it.

I have watched him bunt a baseball and take
not one base but two as he circled round
the fielders like some magician. Just last week
I had to scratch my head when he asked me
if Jesus would also save other human beings
on planet X in some galaxy a hundred light years
hence. Then asked how would we ever know?

Just now this twelve-year-old is plotting how
he's ever going to save up enough walking dogs
to get himself a brand-new Maserati.
I have watched him watching his father's
every move, especially since his father's stroke
three years back, how he's always there
for him, like some pint-sized guardian angel,
there to pull the demons from his father's back
and grab them by their collars to send them out
the door even as he lets his good dog Coal,
who's whining now, back into the house
and family fold to be held and petted once again.

II

MEXICO

It will be the last time the U.S. Cavalry
will use horses in combat. Spads, Fokkers,
machine guns, tanks will shortly see to that.
My grandfather is nineteen and hails from
Paterson, the filthy Passaic the river
he knows best. Now it's the Rio Grande
that greets him and his Army issue horse
whose name is Red. That much I know.
Harry. Harry Szymborski or Sembeski
or Sembooki, or however the census takers
spelled his name, what the hell difference
did it make? His parents worked the mills
along the Falls as weavers and machinists,
grinding work, and why he joined the Army.
Five eight, brown eyes, brown hair, bantam
weight, so the records say. In the black and white
photo I have of him he's excised his face
so the eye can focus on his horse.

It's April 1916, and he's part of the Expedition
going after Villa. He's saddled up and his carbine
glints, and soon he will he heading south
from Texas into Mexico after a shadow
the Army will never capture. Through endless arid
days and deserts, past blossoming cacti
and blue fevered skies and serpentine arroyos,
past the chalk-dry bones of men and cattle
flowing ghostlike backward by him,
he floats as in a dream, the language strange
and those who live there stranger, one
more U.S. soldier awakening to another
twilight nightmare: Okinawa, the Chosin
Reservoir, Khe Sanh and Kuwait's smoldering
oil fields, then Kabul, until at last one arrives
once more in JubJub Land, one more Polish kid
following orders, one more benighted knight

sent out to make the world safe, at least for oil,
trudging back to Texas, then on to France,
where mustard gas will get him, having done
his part to end the war to end all wars until
the next one calls, and then the next, and
the twilit borders bleed together, as he goes on
doing what he must, until at last the very road
he rides upon with Red his horse will have
long since turned to dust along with him.

UNCONCH
For Martín Espada

There he is, his left hand over Unconch's shoulder.
He's smiling, my father, while Unconch stares
into the camera, looking like he'd as soon
punch you in the mouth as speak to you.

This was a year before my father met
my mother and got her pregnant with yours truly,
you understand. A wise guy's world, this,
the fancy 1930 eight-cylinder Oakland

Sedan they've been working on this hot
summer afternoon in '38,
that stand of sycamores like some Greek chorus
in the background doubling the eerie silence.

And look: sepia-black grease stains smearing
my father's coveralls and Unconch's polo shirt
and face like warpaint. And there's that wrench clenched
in my father's right hand. Never mind that I have

no idea what happened to Unconch since that day,
or that I never bothered to ask my father how Unconch
(no last name) got that wacky moniker.
Was it slang for the Unconscious? Was Unconch

some unwitting harbinger of Freud's Surrealists?
And would Unconch have punched me in the mouth
for trying to be a wise-ass by even mentioning
a friggin' woid like Surrealism to him. . .

or to tell the truth even to my father?
In the neighborhood where I grew up,
just as in theirs, you didn't mouth words
like Surreal if you knew what was good

for you, or try on irony by saluting a guy
like Unconch, who would have just stared
back at you, surreal-like, because that's just
what both our worlds were. Words, you learn

early, come at a price. You learn early too
when to use them, when not. As Unconch
and my father would have known, both of whom
long ago returned to silence, as we all will,

every last word—dull or bright or blazing—de-
composing into ten billion pixels, all floating off
into the surf's horizon, the way a conch held too
long to your ear slips finally from your hand.

PANTOUM FOR EAST FIFTY-FIRST

And then, in an instant, it's gone: the world of East Fifty-First.
Gone the round-the-clock clack of the Third Avenue El,
the clutch-grinding rattle of Fords and the clop clop
of those gray dun drayhorses down on the cobblestone street.

Gone now the demon-like sparkles and screams of the El
that mixed with the curses of street kids on the sidewalk below.
Gone too the hunchbacked ragman on that flint-filthy street,
and old Mr. Quinn muttering curses, sweeping the stoop.

Gone the shouts of the gang on that sad sidewalk below,
German and Irish, most of them, a wolf pack with little to do
except toss insults at Quinn, as he went on sweeping the stoop
or tarring the roof or stoking the coal and banking the furnace.

Irish and German, offspring of immigrants, who demanded their due
from whomever they could, like my six-year-old self,
as I fled, the one guinea kid on the block, and hid by the furnace,
a furnace in embryo myself as they doused me with cold kerosene.

Back from the movies under the El, my Brer Rabbit self,
humming *zip-a-dee-doo-dah* while they torched Christmas trees
dumped on the street, then doused me with cold kerosene,
as my mother ran toward me screaming, and they scattered and fled.

Cold fear glimpsed by the light of those crackling trees. . .
And the synagogue cantor handing out seedcakes and bread,
then Harry hurtling the bread back at the old man as we fled.
The pity and fear of it, oh, and the gift of that bread.

And the go-cart Quinn built me and Harry broke, and the bread.
And the gang on the tar-blackened roof back those seventy years,
unfurling the flag with the swastika on it. Oh, and the gift of the bread.
And me in my First Communion tie and knickers that May.

And Harry teaching us love words back those seventy years,
when he ordered Bobby and me to jiggle up down, up down.
And me on my roof in those spiffy black knickers that May,
and my father slamming Harry's brother in his wife beater's shirt

when he'd had it with Harry and the brother went down.
Gone, all gone now, along with the faint cries of the Third Avenue El,
and the sullen Fords and the blood-smeared wife beater's shirt,
and the dray horses fading west down East Fifty-First.

JOHNNIE WALKER BLACK

And there he is, in the fishscale light
of morning up on East 65th.
It's 1945 and our mother
has walked my little brother Walter

and me to this decaying brownstone
to visit the widow of my father's cousin,
Frank, whose Army Jeep crashed somewhere
in Germany just weeks before. Margie

is her name, and she's left now with two young
boys: Frankie, whose father never had a chance
to hold him, and who will come to share
an attic room with Walter and myself.

And then there's Frankie's brother, who has
just squeezed out through the kitchen
window onto the bleak back yard, stepping
on one of the babe chicks he's gone out to feed.

And now he's howling with yet another loss.
But then that's neither here nor there now,
is it? For even then you knew such missteps
could never be undone. And so with the one

who writes these words, standing there
with Walter by some bent garbage can
down the darkened street, as he rifles through
a box of stale cupcakes the grocer has just

tossed into the ashcan as if it were some
newfound grail. But when Walter demands
some crumbs, his brother grabs an empty
whiskey bottle from the grail and brings it

hard down across his mouth and then blood
is gushing out and there's a black gap
where Walter's front teeth were. And now
our mother is on the curb shrieking

for a cab to stop please stop and then
my brother's gone, leaving another gap
as black as hell itself. And here's the thing:
you spend a lifetime trying to understand

just what it was you did that morning. But all
you can piece together is that sullen garbage
can, illumined by a flickering tongue of light
coming from the grocery window. That,

and a black bottle that seems to snigger
at what you have accomplished. And here's
another thing. Walter and I still joke about
that whiskey bottle all these decades later,

and always over a bottle of Johnnie Walker Black,
Walter's favorite, served straight up for him
in a crystal tumbler, repentant Cain offering it
as Walter takes it with that capped-tooth grin

of his, both of us laughing at what happened
way back when in a world long gone, the first shot
followed by another and another, Cain trying
to make amends for what can never be amended.

IN THE REALM OF KINGS AND QUEENS

Seventy years on and the scene still screams.
We've just crossed over the 59th Street Bridge
only to descend into the shrieking malebolge

they call Long Island City. It's nineteen
forty-seven and we're bump bumping
along under the wingèd crosshatched humping

shadows above the spittle-gray cobblestones,
past the grim brick factories as if underwater.
The glint of trolley rails, Fords and Chevies moaning

and yawing this way then that, the stuttering grind
of oil and coal trucks muscling in from everywhere.
My mother—she's still in her early twenties—

stares straight ahead, trying hard as even I can see
to concentrate on driving through this nightmare.
My brother Walter, feet dangling, sits here

in the back-seat tense across from me, and little
Emely, burbling, is saddled to the seat between.
I stare out the left rear window at the blare

of traffic. No radio. Just the roar of angry horns,
when suddenly, like that, from out of nowhere,
a monster cement truck comes slicing over, no warning,

just the exposed nuts of that gargantuan wheel
chewing up the left front door and fender
of our pre-War Ford, like some demon out of hell.

Of course she has no choice now but to pull over
to the crumbling curbside, as the sullen truck pulls
over too, and then the cab door opens, and the driver

is yelling at my mother, demanding to know
where she ever learned to friggin' drive, and no,
no, he ain't taking no blame, lady, for none

of this shit, you understand? *You unnerstan'?*
And there's my mother, trembling for the safety
of her kids, saying something at the looming man,

trying to reason where there's no room for reason
because there's no cop anywhere to be seen.
And then he's off and gone, and we're heading home

to greet our father, who, when he sees the damage done,
makes it clear he's pissed. And there's the lesson, son,
you've learned: that it's a man's world, you understand?

It's men who make the rules by which we're bound
and by which the world turns: a wheel roaring up on
you, as it just goes grinding round and round. And round.

MRS. G'S LESSON PLAN

With a little taste of this
and a little taste of that. . .
That afternoon I took a pint-sized
carton off the milk truck
parked behind the cafeteria
of the Island Trees Middle School

to show my fellow sixth graders
I was one of them (though I
was not) and how the driver stormed
out and snatched it back (which I
was going to put back anyway)
and how Mrs. G (for whom

a school was shortly after named)
said *she* would handle this, and how
her steelrimmed glasses searched
me over with that ice cold
glint of hers and told me come up
here come up *now* in front of the class,

here by the blackboard and clapped
her hands and barked class, class,
and everyone looked up and then,
after an infinity or so, growled that
this was what a (pint-sized) thief
looked like and I turned around

to see who she could have meant.
Then, seeing it was me, scurried back
to my seat, me, the thief, my sorry tail
between my legs *with a little taste*
of this and a little taste of that. . .
In witness thereof the said branding

took place in the spring of Anno
Domini 1951.
I'd just turned eleven, the youngest
in the class, having skipped a grade
way back, and though my angel teacher
could not know it then, the gates

of Eden shut, as I became the youngest
among the boys who went on getting big
and bigger. They say there are always
lessons to be learned, both in and out
of books. There's Basho, Dante, Maimonides,
and Rilke, and then there's Augustine

with his tale about those pears he stole
then simply tossed away, all of whom
taught me things, though nothing like what
you did back then, my dear Mrs. G,
*with a little taste of this and a little
taste of that,* all them many moons ago.

WHEN MY FATHER FOUND OUT I WROTE POETRY

we were on our way down
to Camp Baumann in Merrick
it was the summer of '56
he pulled the dump truck over
to the side off Old Country Road
turned off the engine and gripped
both hands around the steering wheel
I hear you're writing (there was a slight
pause and then he spat out the word)
poetry is it true he wanted to know
there was another pause this time mine
I'd written a poem or two and I was
thinking to myself holy crap what do
I do now caught as I was then I said
yes I had but really it was no big deal
well he said in a low voice you're still
my son and then he turned the key
and the engine started up and soon
we were back on the road heading south
and me about to start another day
gathering the golden droppings
of Bob Baumann's horses in their Pegasian
stables down by the pines relieved
to know I was still my father's son.

MOTHERS' DAY, 2019

We were headed north up 91, my wife
behind the wheel, me in the passenger's seat
the better to hear her. Mother's Day and raining—
as it had been for the past week. We'd driven
down to West Springfield for brunch, the grandkids—
two elevens, a fourteen, a fifteen, a seventeen—
together with two of our sons and their wives.
Even our Jesuit son, out in San Jose
teaching Chinese, seemed with us in spirit.

Despite the frigid downpour, it felt like
a re-enactment of Da Vinci's Last Supper:
Eileen at the head and flowers for the mothers
and love and laughter. And when Eileen asked us
to remember something special about our mothers
my joking ceased as I replayed the story
of how my father'd meant to pull me out
of school when I turned sixteen to work full
time in that Sinclair station across from
the courthouse in Mineola, what with six
kids to feed and money scarce, which was what
he'd had to do back in the Depression.

Which was when my mother, gone now, God
rest her soul, these thirty years and more,
told him straight out the only way
that was ever going to happen was over
her dead body. And to tell the truth, there must've been
something to the way she said it because
he dropped the subject and let it go at that.
And saying that to that man, friend, took courage.
I had meant to tell a funny ha ha story,
you understand, but suddenly I was weeping
and my grandkids were hugging me as I
wiped my eyes and muttered something
though for the love of me I can't remember what.

What I do remember is the sense of dovelike
comfort that seemed to blanket me as I
looked over at Eileen who has always been there
for me even when I wasn't there for her.
And here's the thing: driving home, the two
of us, the rain seemed to caress the maples
all along the highway, each leaf and bush
and blade of grass blazing now with grace.

III

III

THOSE SHIFTING SANDS
For Natasha Trethewey

The black guide at Fort Sumter thirty years ago,
waving vaguely out toward the gray Atlantic.
In a low & steady voice he says, yes, they're still
out there somewhere in the shifting sands,

but washed under, like so much of our history.
Having driven down from New York, I'd asked
him for the best way out to Fort Wagner,
where Colonel Shaw and the colored troops

of the Massachusetts Fifty-Fourth charged
the rebel mounds one July night back
in 1863, their bullet-battered bodies dragged
and gathered, then tossed into some makeshift grave.

They're all gone now, all without a marker:
spattered wood, diced bone, rusting muzzle,
somewhere out there beneath those roiling waves.
I've been to Charleston half a dozen times,

and love the food there, especially the oysters
and the minty juleps. Love too the halcyon view
of the harbor from the park which lies South
of Broad, flanked by those antebellum houses

which somehow survived Sherman's blitzkrieg.
Love too the oak-lined drive among the patched
Gone with the Wind plantations that fan out to the north.
I've climbed the parapets at Moultrie, where Sergeant

Major Edgar Allan Poe, trapped, brooded among
the drizzle and mosquitoes. Though that
was years before Beauregard twirled
his black mustachios, preparing to unleash

all hell on Sumter and his old instructor
from his West Point days and watch Old Glory
flicker a final time amid the fireworks.
Then too there's *Glory,* with Denzel

Washington and Morgan Freeman, and
the late Shelby Foote to advise them
on how all that death went down.
But to measure all of that against those grim

blue-black soldiers in Union jackets
marching forward double time, then charging
the rebel redoubts as if ascending some lost Skull
Hill, as they headed straight into that hail

of hissing mini-balls to show a wounded nation
how it might reshape itself. Think potter's clay.
Think blood-drenched soft sift stirring up
the shifting sands of history even as they sank.

THE GREAT MISSISSIPPI
For Philip Kolin

Raised on the mean streets of New York City,
my earliest memories are of another river
altogether. Hardly a river, really, that gray-green
slick of prairie flowing southward from the tiny park
off Fifty-first. Or the same river glimpsed
from the Queens side, two blocks off Rainey Park,
where my Nona lived with her one living
daughter and her family back during the war.
The river that is East: a lake-like salty current that slides
south beneath the tugboats and barges roiling through it
until it loses itself where the greenbronze Colossus we call
Liberty beckons with her beacon-like torch, a curriculum
that still somehow enfolds the shadow of my mother.

Or the river to the west that sweeps beneath
the great GW with its incessant traffic, up which
Hudson sailed in search of the nonexistent Northeast
Passage 400 years ago. Or that same river, even more
majestic, flowing south at Beacon, across from
Washington's winter quarters, and where I spent a year
in prayer and quizzing thought in the old stone blockhouse
torn down all those years ago in the name of progress.

For the past forty-five years it has been the Connecticut,
the Long River, glowing with the late summer sun among
the maples at the bend where Montague meets Sunderland,
or the same river at the earliest end of March as it winds
its way past Hartford and Haddam toward the Sound.

But the Great River, the mythic one with real cliffs
and riverbanks to whelm a boy from Levittown
was the great Mississippi, flowing through his soul
still vividly in that one-room schoolhouse in old Bethpage
among the oaks back in '49, when he rode the river with Tom

and Huck and Jim there in his creaking wooden seat,
all the world before him as they reclined there musing
on the makeshift bobbing raft and smoked an imaginary corncob
pipe, as—thirty years later—his own boys would ride the Long
River in a makeshift raft as their father watched them from the shore.

I have seen the Mississippi, alone and with them, north
from where it flows below the high bridge at Minneapolis,
when Henry wrote his last Dream Song—one line short—
before he waved goodbye in the howling winter wind
and tilted over, thirsting for its waters. Have seen the river
dotted with its sandy islands at Hannibal, and at St. Louis
beneath the arches and the bobbing river barges.

Have seen it too at Vicksburg, where the skeletons
of river boats long came to rest, and past Bourbon Street
along the levees, when its muddy bosom turned golden
in the sunset. And for all men have done to wound it,
it is still a holy river in the glimmers it gives off like grace
at the most unexpected times. A song then for the tribes
who fished along its banks, for the French fathers who
later fished for souls there. A song too for the cardsharps
and piano players riding the great sternwheelers,
and for the restless shadows of our black brothers
searching for a way out or down.

                                    De Soto's man, beholding
the swollen river at what once was the site of Aminoya, calling it
"a beautiful thing to look upon, this sea that had been fields,
with only the tips of the tallest trees still visible,"
some strong brown god, waiting, watching and waiting.
"I stood like one bewitched," Twain remembered. "A broad
expanse of the river was turned to blood," which brightened
into graceful circles and lines of radiating gold, until—when he
tried to make it his did all the grace, the beauty, and
the poetry leave it. Only in the imagination, one comes to see,
does the river flow on in crystal, as on a raft piloted by a boy,
or an old man resting in an armchair, dreaming of its waters.

VIEUX CARRÉ

As if you left the theater "with the impression
of having been told a secret. Not a truth,
but a secret." Clive Barnes for the *New York Times,*
summing up Tennessee Williams's late play, which saw
five performances before they shut the doors.

Williams, at 65, trying to understand his own
misbegotten youth, the early glory of some streetcar
named *Desire* long behind him then, the downward
spiral as of some French wrought iron grille rusting
in the unforgiving summer heat. Such beauty, such

plangent beauty he must have seen all about
the Vieux Carré, the jazz-saturated air, the blues,
the palpable sorrow of the helpless gambler who wages
everything and loses. The crowds at Mardi Gras,
the bands, the cheap and glittering trinkets tossed by angel-

headed feathered figures from the floats, the rain-soaked
cemeteries with their rotting dead, the faithful few
at dawn on Ash Wednesday heading for the cathedral
on the square. The mud layers of its history: Huguenots,
red coats advancing, then Union gunboats, the miasma,

the old slave quarters with their chains, Preservation
Hall and Louis Armstrong's gravelly voice which
knocked them dead. The delta waters rising as Katrina
struck, Tremé, the cops disappearing or taking what
they could. And the tropic light you caught there

in the quiet courtyard, as in Paris or the land
of *langue d'oc.* Faulkner, Cable, Degas, Kate Chopin,
Rice's homebred vampirism and the living dead
who wander Bourbon Street. Mahalia Jackson's
Gospel music, Joe King Oliver, the genius of Marsalis,

and of course the Voodoo Queen, Marie Laveau.
You walk these streets, you, some misplaced Yankee
from New York, and dine on chargrilled oysters and sip
your bourbon, then leave the theater, wondering what
the secret is they keep, knowing that you'll never know.

MARDI GRAS SEEN FROM THE OUTSIDE

Late winter 1995.
And here we are, my wife and I, Hartford
to New Orleans, staying at a small hotel
with friends off Bourbon Street, four Yankee
pilgrims come to witness for ourselves
this thing called Mardi Gras and all that jive,
this Fat Tuesday that at midnight will blend
into the astringent fasts of Ash Wednesday
and the forty days of Lent. Or does it anymore?

Or is this really all there is: downing yet
another hurricane or one more julep
or an absinthe or, ah yes, a Sazerac,
while one more drunky college girl undoes
her jersey and lets it all hang out (unlike Juliet)
on that spectral balcony across the Way?
Have we come all this way to merely feast
on gumbo (*laissez les bons temps rouler!*),
or jambalaya, or a bowl of crawfish étouffée?

Ah, but what of the lost off to the side?
The beggars begging, the con-men who masquerade
as seasoned guides to show you some fake
French Quarter? Or worse, the murphy men,
the pickpockets, the cops on the take?
And what of the dead who have stayed dead
all these many years in these dark cemeteries
just off the beaten path with their mausoleums
and crumbling stones among the live oak trees?

Still, what I remember most is that small, thin
black man with his sad face, a minstrel
I guess you'd say, who'd entered through
an exit door while I was feasting and began
to sing and strum his beat-up banjo and. . .
But it was all so sad, and I found myself weeping
as he strummed a tune I can't recall. A face,
but the face of the Delta, an *Ecce Homo* face,
a face like Christ's, the face of a brown man beaten,

spat upon, then mocked and lynched, but who'd
survived, trudging through centuries of Lents
without Fat Tuesdays, a man who would rise again
to sing his song and make it (as it was meant
to be) ours too, those gospel blues (thanks to Fats
and Louis and Jelly Roll, and Elvis too, I'd guess,
who drank so much from them). And while it's true
that the Yankee outsider remains outside, for a blessed
moment something like a light broke through.

THE SICK MAN

He was coming back it was a long way yet
and the narrow passage was dark
but there was a light dim and hovering ahead
he knew what being on the edge of life
was like now and he wanted life wanted
breath air light love he was not
very coherent yet that much he knew
but he wanted to think more clearly
to behold once more the blossoms
on the ancient catalpa in his yard
as they fell in the breeze like
a gentle snow and pick the white
orchid-shaped things up by the handful
and rub their grapey perfume gently
against his nose and breathe in the sweet
earth again and again and please God again

COMING BACK FROM THE DEAD

can be disconcerting take it from one
who's been there hobbling on rubber legs
through fifty shades of graves to end up
riding down a metal tunnel that kept screeching
ha! haha! ha! your body strapped to a gurney

where *(ha ha!)* if you blinked the whole insane
scenario would have to be re-played and where,
at the nightmare hour, exhausted and confused,
you might almost be forgiven if you let
your guard down as I did one dark night

after weeks of drifting sideways down
the lonesome corridors of the indifferent hospital.
Surely the stone-faced technician
hunched over the demented ill-lit controls
had to be a Mossad agent or was he

KGB or CIA
or Walsingham the Queen's spy,
with a wrecked Jesuit wracked there
on the twisting ropes I can't say for sure
except that that's what paranoia does to you.

So, where's this going? this nightmare scene
that will not let me be? And now it's back to those
chiaroscuro corridors where they will close me
round and drill into my skull shunting
wires down my spine to fine-tune my sick brain

so it can rise again at last from the long dark night
it has spent these last months entombed in
and follow the flicker of what I take to be
an eastering light. . .me, there, among the crocuses,
all three of them, and all a lovely purple.

PSALM FOR THE LOST

Down the dark way, the dark way down.
Everything dark now, as he has come to see:
that the way was always dark, the journey dark,
the mind dark, the answers like the questions
dark, each day dark, the glaucous pearl white eyes,
even when the sun spread across the greengold grass,
glistening the bright skin of the copper beeches.

Dark, dark, and dark. Because it is the nature
of the restless mind which knows too well
that nothing is ever really known, no matter
how much one tells oneself it is. The books,
the words: all so much straw, even when
they seemed to blaze with meaning. One
more piece, he used to think, one more shard

to complete the puzzle, even as it all
slipped down the drain, the vortex
of the drain, dark, dark, and dark. And it was night,
John says, the light departed, the face distorted
in the brazier's glow. I know him not. Yes,
I knew him once, and the sunlight sang. But that
was then, you have to understand. That was then,

before the answers like the very questions ceased
to call out to each other. Yes, that was then, when I built
my castle by the sea in the bright mid-morning sun,
and thought that what I'd made was good, before
the indifferent tide came rolling in again, dissolving
everything. Dark, dark, oh dark. And nothing for it
but to let the wind rebuild it, bit by bit, and lift it as it will.

HORNETS' NEST

"I really feel I can touch you even in this darkness when I pray."
James Foley (1973-2014) from his last message to his family

"Man Jack the man is, just" Gerard Manley Hopkins

Recovered now enough to scrub the deck,
which turned dun brown with insidious dirt
and cobwebs in the months I twisted, hurt-
ing in yet one more hospital bed, my spine a wreck,

my wobbling brain awash in static bubbles
instead of what I used to tell myself were tough,
astringent thoughts. Oh, Lord, they say, the troubles
I've seen. Well, Jack, get over that self-pity stuff.

Your dear wife has a job for you to do,
so do it. Soap & water (warm works best),
a sponge, a piston stream of water and, Jack, you
have it! Progress! Until you spray a hidden nest

of hornets, who come at you, each a fighter plane
zigging this way, then that, to catch you by surprise
as your left wrist then your right foot erupt in pain.
And now they've found your face, and both your eyes,

and you beat what the Brits call a hasty retreat.
But dammit this is *your* porch, *your* house, *your* home,
and if these S.O.B.s had just remained discreet
or—better—stayed hidden in their aerodrome

you might have done the live let live. But no! Not now.
This is war, and either you or they will have to go.
And so you grab two cans of Raid and POW!
And it's right in the kisser, as Gleason would say. Hel*lo*

my pretty ones! By now I'm hornet mad myself, and keep
hitting them with everything I've got. And *they* hit back
with everything *they've* got. Worse, they have deep
reserves, as one winged fiend multiplies by twenty, Jack.

And soon you're like Cuchulain swinging at the sea
as wave on wave keeps coming in. And in the end
you know you cannot win, though you win this round. Be
there when they swarm me, You, my first, fast, last Friend.

ON LUCA SIGNORELLI'S SELF-ANOINTED ONES

Try as he did to get it right, he seemed to get it wrong.
Name wrong, place wrong, wrong town, wrong state,
wrong word, wrong tone, wrong stress, wrong map, wrong date:
golem errors that told him he was wrong and wrong.
And now the keepers of the word there to prolong
the torture: samurais dispensing their cloacal fate
as they pursed their lips, burbling what to love and hate.
Wrong, wrong, because he'd dared to sing his song.

Others seemed kinder, merely condescending
to point out where he'd missed the mark, though
when they'd skewed him through, at least were kind
enough to lift their jackboots from his neck, pretending,
as they wiped their visors and their swords, to know
how they alone, blind mouths, were fit to lead the blind.

JEFF EXPLAINS THE POETRY OF MONEY
(WITH SOME ADDED WISDOM FROM WALTER)

For my friend, Jeff Affeldt

"Money is a kind of poetry." —Wallace Stevens
"Money talks. Nobody walks." —Walter Mariani

Here's what the magic man told me,
the guy who's been there for me
for forty years now, the guy who loves
his wife and kids as I do mine, the guy
with the fast car, which he revs up
in my driveway as he peels away, the guy
who talks cash, the man with the moola,
the guy with the big shoulders, who loves
fresh scones and knows how to knead dough
for those who need dough, the guy who makes
what they call in the business bread.
Well, friends, here's what he said:
"Listen. I know how to pull dineros out of a hat.
Make shekels, mazuma, bucks, greenbacks, cash,
yeah, hard cash, cold cash, ready money, funny money.
I'm the magician with the means, man.
You know, the wherewithal, the funds, the capital,
the fuzzy finance stuff, the coins, the change,
high-o silver, currency that's flowing like a river,
remuneration, emolument, bills, notes, wealth,
specie, pelf, lucre (filthy it is NOT!).
I be the man who watches over your monthly
statements like a hawk. A veritable guardian angel
I am, the guy who duly notes "all moneys paid
into and out of your accounts." I'm the man
who watches your assets *and* your ass.
Money, money, money. What some folks
marry (or kill) for. You say you wanna know
how it all goes down? Look at this chart.
Note how the scamaramus intersects

per annum with the variable flabafloobus.
Got it? Made myself clear? Better still,
jus' leave it to all to Jeff the Magic Man.
Just keep those scones comin' my way.
And listen to what your brother has to say:

(*Walter enters stage left*):
Well, they say the best things in life are free
But you can give all that to the birds and the bees.
I want money (money). That's what I want,
Oh yeah, money, that's what I need.

 They say love can give us some kinda thrill.
But love don't pay all them blanking bills.
I want money. Money! That's what I want!
That's the stuff to fill up on, Phil.

They say money can't buy everything, that's true.
But what it can't buy you can have. Me, I want revenue!
Money. That's what I want, Mr. Jeff. Money!
Money rainin' down from outta the blue!
I want money. Moola, moola, moola,
I want money. Yeah, money,
Jeff, baby. What I crave is money!

Exit right, first Jeff, then Walter, then Pablo, led by a carrot.

IV

MITZVAH

A Saturday night, late February. Eileen and me
in the back of the cramped car, Julie driving,
Bruce riding shotgun. We're heading down
to Amherst for an evening of Borscht Belt vaudeville,
Fifty Shades of Oy Vey at the local Jewish temple,
and Julie's taking all the back roads, so that, though
I've lived here for fifty years, I'm already lost,
when we see a car stopped, lights dimmed,
stranded at a crossing like some lost sheep.

Julie stops, pulls over, walks over to the car, knocks
on the window and asks the driver—a woman in her eighties—
if she's alright. It takes her a while to answer, her voice low.
"I, I think I'm lost," she stutters. "I was visiting
my daughter, as, as I have so many times, but now
I'm lost and don't know where I am or what to do."

All this is taking time, precious time, you have to understand,
and meanwhile I want to get a move on to where the fun is
and hear some Jewish jokes. In fact I've got one myself.
This blond broad—a goy—is at a Jewish wedding
and the waiter serves her soup. "What's this," she asks,
and the waiter says, "Madam, this is matzoh ball soup,"
and the blond looks down, then up, and says, "Do you have
some other part of the matzoh you could serve me?"

A joke no doubt followed by a rim shot off the snare
"Bah da dum." Instead, here we are, in the middle
of who the hell knows where, and Julie's trying
her best to calm the woman, telling her to follow us
down to the package store over by the railroad tracks
so the woman can call her daughter—embarrassed
by the fact she's lost—and get her safely home. And
to make matters worse, the woman can't remember
her daughter's number, until finally she does.

But Julie won't leave her till she gets the daughter
on the phone, who says she's out the door and coming.
And the young woman, who was just closing up
the store for the evening, says she'll wait and make sure
the poor woman's picked up and sees her on her way.
She can leave her car there overnight so the daughter
can rest easy and drive her mother home. That's it, and
we're finally good to go and get down to the temple.

Three women—four, if you count my wife—all
anxious to see the episode resolved and the woman
safe again, and me, internally rehearsing the joke
about the blond to get the timing right and hear
the laughter and a clap or two. And then of course
it hits me, that what I've just witnessed is a mitzvah
(though I confuse that with a mikvah, a Jewish bath,
which is like me). But no, this is a genuine mitzvah
I've just witnessed, there on a dark road among
the shadows and the stark maples, which even now
have begun to pulsate with the sap of life again,
and though I surely don't deserve it, I've just been
blessed again by another random act of kindness,
something heartfelt, something real, this—how
do you say it?—this loving your neighbor
as yourself, someone nameless and confused and, yes,
embarrassed. Someone as lost as your sorry self.

THE SILENCE OF THOSE SHADOWS

There were trees and then there were
more trees. First the copper beech
and the angel-headed flowering catalpa.
And the road kept going south, past
the pond there in the shadows, where
something keeps kindly watch for me.

There was a flash of road and then another
and another, each one going under,
as the mowed fields disappeared
off Forty-seven. Then a left turn onto
Sixty-three, past Gunn Road, then on
past Federal, as I have come and gone

a thousand times and more, those years
I drove south to meet my students, their faces
ever-changing with the seasons. And then
more trees. Those maples, oaks, and pines,
which I never stopped for, though they have stopped
all these years for me. Blue spruce, yes,

and hemlock, and those quaking aspens, what
Mitch who built our kitchen called his popples.
Black walnuts too, and spruce and elm, and
that lone surviving chestnut standing by
the roadside day and night, though I was
too busy then to get where I had to be to see.

And on, past those nameless rock outcroppings:
quartz, granite, gneiss, and sandstone, and the almond-
speckled schist, coarse pegmatite, mica
traprock, feldspar: things that have been here
a hundred million years and more, give or take
the eyeblink fourscore I have come to call my own.

The fevered Sixties and the war in Nam.
Flying out of La Fleur with my stalwart
colleagues across the Sound to LaGuardia
to teach comp classes to my Black TAs
in Bedford-Stuy, the Cessna cutting far
too close for comfort over the Whitestone Bridge

as we flew back in winter darkness
to follow once again the outline of the river valley
that has been my home these fifty years, most
of those who sat beside me ghosts now, Charlie
lauding the splendors of *Tristram Shandy* while I prayed
as the fragile plane came bouncing down the runway.

So many ghosts. And I, still here to bid
farewell to those who left our "Happy Valley,"
as we called it then, those men and women
who found this life too hard to deal with and now
are gone, either somewhere near, or in some stranger
place to try and understand what here they couldn't.

And yes, yes, the place has changed, as places will,
either in the name of "progress," or sometimes
to return to something like they were before,
as the trees, those silent guardians standing there
over in the shadows, as they keep waiting for me
to finally see them for what and who they were.

WHAT THE WAVES KEPT TELLING ME

Mighty waters cannot quench love
Nor can floods sweep it away.

    Song of Solomon 8:6

We were somewhere off the coast of Sweden,
the land my mother's mother's family had sailed from
all those years ago. A cruise. My wife, my oldest son,
myself. Mid-morning, and I kept staring into the sea
below us, mesmerized by the wake the liner made,

how wave after wave after wave kept forming
before each fell back, the luminescent foam
coalescing as if somehow held together,
then breaking up bit by bit by bit,
until each seemed to disappear forever.

I kept thinking of the strange dream I'd had
months before, my body burnt and turned
to ash, how the dust seemed to float now
somewhere in a dark and alien space
as on a wave somehow held together, unlike

the waves I was watching now, for a distant light
seemed there to hover over what was left of me.
And I knew now there was nothing those particles
could do, that if they were ever to coalesce
and rise again, it would have to be by the hand

(hand? yes, hand is what I thought) of the Father
(yes, the one he'd called his Father, his and mine)
who would lift me up and somehow make us whole
again, my family, my wife, my son, smiling now
as I turned to wave at them as they drew nearer.

A DISTANT PURPLE
For H.M. March 6, 1923–September 16, 1988

Mid-September, dear woman, and the monarch
lights once more upon the purple panoplied
butterfly bush in the now-decaying garden,
as it has for the past thirty Septembers.

And once again, like the softest breeze, I feel
your gentle presence and lift my open hand
toward it, toward you, hoping for a sign, me,
your firstborn, who never seemed to have

the time while you were with us still.
My hand unfolds, the monarch hovering,
before it turns to float across the garden
to another bush to settle there instead.

And still I wait, wondering if it, if you,
might rise from the distant purple and return
here by my open trembling hand and settle,
if only for a moment, dear woman, before

you lift and travel to some distant land
as monarchs will. How you loved butterflies,
so much so I had one etched on your gravestone
when you left us that September, having given us

all you had before the cancer took you, took you
ah! too soon. Remember that final phone call,
your voice already tired, when I said I'd be there?
I said. I said. Then driving north through the rain-

soaked night, getting lost and more lost as on
we drove, then getting there too late. Stay now,
mother, stay just a little longer, before you're
off again, bound for some other place called home.

ON THE WAY HOME

there was a moment
we were coming down
from the turbulent waters
of the Maligne it had been
raining for what seemed
hours on end there was
a thick mist hanging in the air,
a billowing high above
the larches and the pines
so that the mountain peaks
seemed all but hidden
when suddenly without warning
the face of one mountain
far off to our left began
to shine it was as if
some mystery had just revealed
the merest glimpse of what it was.

I thought of Peter bartering
with Jesus on the Mount
of Transfiguration to stay, stay,
or Moses alone there on the Mountain
as the wind whispered
in all but words here I am
immerse yourself in me now,
now, for even this must pass
and you will descend, returning
to a world which will or will not
care. But know too that this moment
may well return and it will be
as if we came together then
forever and for good.

THEY TOO GO ROUND

In Williams's *Pictures from Breughel* they go round
and around, those peasants pounding the ground
with their clogs and their boots to the sound
of the fiddles and sackbuts. True, nothing profound

there, just a rollicking midsummer dance with the stout-
rumped male and female, those suds-sodden faces caught
in a moment both comic and sad. But haven't we all thought
of ourselves, our own lives circling round and about

in time's turning, atuning, aturning, left hand
and right reaching out in a wheel like the spheres
in their own solemn round dance, pivoting round
like wheels circling some invisible maypole, at its center

a ringdance of the blessèd, the way Fra Angelico
reveals in his *Judgment,* that angelic choir gazing as if into
your soul as others gaze upward, the radiant glow
of that sea-changing moment, now and forever, *hoy hoya ho.*

Remember the wheel at the Tuileries those long years
ago? The fear as you stared down into the dark? Or your steer-
ing wheel locking, as if gripped by some angel, that car
heading for you before it somehow veered off? The sheer

terror of that, then the awe and relief? Or the truck pound-
ing its way into your poor mother's car, the sick sound
as it shredded the door? Oh God, the round of the days, each bound
for oblivion, the hours and minutes going round and around,

reminding us daily of what must come in the end? *Timor
mortis conturbat me,* sings the old song, replaying the fear
that winds and unwinds? Ah, but look! Look as upward they gaze:
 those blessèd, dancing round and around in that circle of praise.

HOLY SATURDAY

A dream the old song has it, just
a dream. I was driving the old beige
Camry going round and around
and around searching for the Jeep
I was sure I'd parked or would have parked
near the decaying wharfs down by the sea
the day before but unable now
to find it though I kept circling back
and forth and back alley after alley
without any luck then finally thought
to press the panic button on my key
fob and yes I thought I could just
make out the beep beep sound
so that I had to believe my car
was waiting out there somewhere
as now fog and night descended.
It was then I remember seeing two
middle-aged women sitting in an old
van one at the foot the other at the head
so I rolled down my window to ask
if they could hear the beep beep
and if they could would they please
please be good enough to tell me
where the signal was coming from
because as I explained my hearing
wasn't very good now and I couldn't tell
if I was even headed in the right direction.
They were friendly enough and both
smiled back at me and asked if it was
a pizza truck or an ambulance
I was looking for or if the thing
was red or white the whole time
these pleasant smiles fitted to their faces
until it dawned on me that I would have to
keep on searching by myself though by now
everything was dark and the signal I was sure

I'd heard I think kept growing dimmer
though it had to be out there oh God
it had to be out there somewhere
still waiting for me to find it.

WHAT HAPPENED THEN

Do we understand what happened then?
The few of us in that shuttered room,
lamps dimmed, afraid of what would happen
when they found us? The women back
this morning to tell Peter what they'd seen.
Then these two back from Emmaus.
And now here he was. Here in the room with us.
Strange meeting this, the holes there
in his hands and feet and heart.
And who could have guessed a calm like this
could touch us? But that was what we felt.
The deep relief you feel when the one
you've searched for in a crowd appears,
and your unbelieving eyes dissolve in tears.
For this is what love looks like and is
and what it does. "Peace"was what he said,
as a peace like no other pierced the gloom
and descended on the room.

Acknowledgments

The author would like to thank the following magazines and anthologies for publishing poems included in this book:

America

The American Journal of Poetry

Arkansas Review

The Best American Poetry 2016

Boston College Magazine

First Things

Goodbye, Mexico: Poems of Remembrance

Image

Philadelphia Poets

Presence: A Journal of Catholic Poetry

The Southern Quarterly: A Journal of the Arts in the South

Spiritus: A Journal of Christian Spirituality

spoKe

This book was set in Perpetua, designed by the British sculptor, artist, and typographer, Eric Gill, in response to a commission in 1925 from Stanley Morrison, an influential historian of typography and adviser to the Monotype foundry. The design for Perpetua grew out of Gill's experience as a stonecarver and the name pays tribute to the early Christian martyr, Vibia Perpetua.

This book was designed by Ian Creeger, Jim Tedrick, and Gregory Wolfe. It was published in hardcover, paperback, and electronic formats by Slant Books, Seattle, Washington.

The cover image is a detail from *Paradise* by Fra Angelico, painted between 1431 and 1435.

www.ingramcontent.com/pod-product-compliance
Lightning Source LLC
Chambersburg PA
CBHW032002060426
42446CB00041B/1247